Grade 4

Making Meaning®

SECOND EDITION

Second edition published 2008.

Making Meaning is a trademark of Developmental Studies Center.

Developmental Studies Center
2000 Embarcadero, Suite 305
Oakland, CA 94606-5300
(800) 666-7270, fax: (510) 464-3670
www.devstu.org

ISBN-13: 978-1-59892-731-3
ISBN-10: 1-59892-731-0

Printed in the United States of America

3 4 5 6 7 8 9 10 MLY 17 16 15 14 13 12 11

Table of Contents

Grade 4

Assessment Overview

The *Assessment Resource Book* is designed to help you make informed instructional decisions and track your students' reading comprehension and social development as you teach the *Making Meaning®* lessons. The expectation in the *Making Meaning* program is that *all* of your students are developing at their own pace into readers with high levels of comprehension, and that they can all develop positive, effective interpersonal skills.

There are three types of assessments in the program: Social Skills Assessments, Class Comprehension Assessments, and Individual Comprehension Assessments. As you follow the lessons in the *Teacher's Manual*, an assessment box will alert you whenever one of these assessments is suggested. The assessment box will also direct you to the corresponding pages in the *Assessment Resource Book*. Each kind of assessment is described briefly below.

Social Skills Assessment

The Social Skills Assessment (SSA) occurs at the end of Units 1, 5, 7, and at the end of the year. This assessment allows you to note how well each student is learning and applying the social skills taught in the program. The SSA record sheet (pages 2–3) allows you to track how students are doing with particular skills over time. The assessment also allows you to track both overall participation in the lessons and how each student integrates the values of responsibility, respect, fairness, caring, and helpfulness into her behavior.

Class Comprehension Assessment

The Class Comprehension Assessment (CCA) is a once-a-week assessment designed to help you assess the performance and needs of the whole class. The CCA usually occurs during guided or independent strategy practice lessons, at a time when the students would be using comprehension strategies they learned during the week. During a CCA, you have the opportunity to randomly observe students as they work in pairs or individually (selecting strong, average, and struggling readers) as you ask yourself key questions. Each week's CCA record sheet (see page 6) gives you space to record your thinking and provides suggestions for how to proceed based on your observations.

Individual Comprehension Assessment

The Individual Comprehension Assessment (ICA) is an end-of-unit assessment designed to help you to assess the comprehension of individual students. The ICA helps you review each student's work and IDR conference notes to see how the students are using strategies and making sense of what they read. Each unit's ICA section (see pages 34–35) provides examples of student work for your reference. You can use the ICA Class Record Sheet (page 48) to track the students' progress over the year.

IDR Conference Notes

Your notes from the IDR conferences you have with students are an important source of information for the ICA. While you do not need to document every IDR conference you have, it is important to document at least one conference per unit per student.

Informal Portfolio Assessment

We suggest that you create individual student folders to collect each student's IDR conference notes, filed chronologically. The *Student Response Book* and the folder comprise an informal portfolio that you can use to discuss the student's progress with the student or others. Before meeting with a student to discuss the portfolio, you might ask him to select one or two pieces of *Student Response Book* work that he feels are examples of good thinking he did while reading and be prepared to talk about this work.

Social Skills Assessment

Social Skills Assessment Record

Use the following rubric to score each student:
1 = does not implement
2 = implements with support
3 = implements independently

STUDENT NAMES

Participates in partner work and class discussions	UNIT 1										
	UNIT 5										
	UNIT 7										
Explains thinking and listens to others	UNIT 1										
	UNIT 5										
	UNIT 7										
Follows classroom procedures *(e.g., moves to read-alouds and class meetings responsibly, observes class meeting ground rules, follows classroom library and independent reading procedures)*	UNIT 1										
	UNIT 5										
	UNIT 7										
Uses "Turn to Your Partner" *(e.g., faces partner, makes eye contact, listens attentively, contributes ideas about the reading, question, or topic)*	UNIT 1										
	UNIT 5										
	UNIT 7										
Uses "Think, Pair, Share" *(e.g., thinks quietly before sharing with a partner)*	UNIT 1										
	UNIT 5										
	UNIT 7										
Is able to reflect on behavior	UNIT 1										
	UNIT 5										
	UNIT 7										
Takes responsibility for own learning and behavior	UNIT 1										
	UNIT 5										
	UNIT 7										
Uses "Think, Pair, Write"	UNIT 5										
Uses prompts to add to others' thinking	UNIT 5										
	UNIT 7										
Agrees and disagrees respectfully	UNIT 5										
	UNIT 7										
Asks clarifying questions	UNIT 5										
	UNIT 7										
Uses "Heads Together" *(e.g., takes turns talking and listening in a group, contributes ideas about the reading, question, or topic)*	UNIT 5										
	UNIT 7										
Includes others	UNIT 5										
	UNIT 7										
Reaches agreement with others	UNIT 7										
Gives reasons for opinions	UNIT 7										
Discusses opinions and gives feedback respectfully	UNIT 7										

																	UNIT 1
																	UNIT 5
																	UNIT 7
																	UNIT 1
																	UNIT 5
																	UNIT 7
																	UNIT 1
																	UNIT 5
																	UNIT 7
																	UNIT 1
																	UNIT 5
																	UNIT 7
																	UNIT 1
																	UNIT 5
																	UNIT 7
																	UNIT 1
																	UNIT 5
																	UNIT 7
																	UNIT 1
																	UNIT 5
																	UNIT 7
																	UNIT 5
																	UNIT 5
																	UNIT 7
																	UNIT 5
																	UNIT 7
																	UNIT 5
																	UNIT 7
																	UNIT 5
																	UNIT 7
																	UNIT 5
																	UNIT 7
																	UNIT 7
																	UNIT 7
																	UNIT 7

Class Comprehension Assessment

Recognizing Text Features—Expository Nonfiction

Observe the class and ask yourself:	All or most students	About half of the students	Only a few students
▸ Do the students notice expository text features?			
▸ Do they have a sense of what information a text feature contributes?			

What to do now:

▸ If **all or most students** are noticing expository text features and seem to have a sense of the information they contribute, proceed with Independent Strategy Practice on Day 4.

▸ If **about half the students** or **only a few students** are noticing text features and seem to have a sense of the information they contribute, you might want to repeat Days 1, 2, and 3 of this week using an alternative book before moving on to Day 4. Alternative books are listed in the Week 1 Overview.

Notes:

Recognizing Text Features—Expository Nonfiction

Observe the students and ask yourself:	All or most students	About half of the students	Only a few students
▸ *Do the students notice expository text features?*			
▸ *Do they have a sense of what information a text feature contributes to the article?*			

What to do now:

▸ If ***all or most students*** are noticing expository text features and seem to have a sense of the information they contribute, proceed with Day 3.

▸ If ***about half the students*** or ***only a few students*** are noticing text features and seem to have a sense of the information they contribute, you might want to repeat Days 1 and 2 of this week using an alternative article before moving on to Day 3. Alternative resources for articles are listed in the Week 2 Overview.

Notes:

Recognizing Text Features—Expository Nonfiction

Observe the students and ask yourself:	All or most students	About half of the students	Only a few students
▶ *Are the students able to recognize all the text features?*			
▶ *Are they able to make sense of the information in the text features?*			

What to do now:

▶ If **all or most students** are able to recognize all the text features and make sense of the information in the text features, proceed with Unit 3.

▶ If **about half the students** or **only a few students** are able to recognize all the text features and make sense of the information in the text features, you might want to repeat this week using an alternative book before moving on to Unit 3. Alternative books are listed in the Week 3 Overview.

Notes:

Questioning—Expository Nonfiction

Observe the students and ask yourself:	All or most students	About half of the students	Only a few students
▶ Are the students able to generate "I wonder" statements?			
▶ Do they use their "I wonder" statements to think about the text?			
▶ Do they refer to the text when discussing their "I wonder" statements?			

What to do now:

▶ If **all or most students** are generating and using "I wonder" statements to think about the text, proceed with the Class Meeting on Day 4 and then continue with Week 2.

▶ If **about half the students** are generating and using "I wonder" statements to think about the text, proceed with Day 4 and then Week 2, and plan to monitor students who are having difficulty. Since this is the first of three weeks of questioning, the students may need more experience with, and modeling of, questioning to become comfortable with it.

▶ If **only a few students** are generating and using "I wonder" statements to think about the text, you might want to repeat Days 1, 2, and 3 of this week using an alternative book before moving on. Alternative books are listed in the Week 1 Overview.

Notes:

Questioning—Expository Nonfiction

Observe the students and ask yourself:	All or most students	About half of the students	Only a few students
▸ Are the students able to ask questions?			
▸ Are their questions relevant to the reading?			
▸ Are they referring to the reading to determine whether their questions have been discussed?			

What to do now:

▸ If **all or most students** are asking relevant questions and referring to the text to determine whether their questions have been discussed, proceed with Week 3.

▸ If **about half the students** are asking relevant questions and referring to the text to determine whether their questions have been discussed, proceed with Week 3 and plan to monitor the students who are having difficulty during independent reading. You might have them read a short passage from their book aloud to you and think of a question they could ask at that point in the reading. Then have them continue reading for a while and check in with them to see whether their question was discussed.

▸ If **only a few students** are asking relevant questions and referring to the text to determine whether their questions have been discussed, you might want to repeat this week using an alternative book before moving on. Alternative books are listed in the Week 2 Overview.

Notes:

Questioning—Expository Nonfiction

Observe the students and ask yourself:	All or most students	About half of the students	Only a few students
▶ *Are the students using references from the text to talk about their questions?*			

What to do now:

▶ If ***all or most students*** are referring to the text to talk about their questions, proceed with Unit 4.

▶ If ***about half the students*** or ***only a few students*** are referring to the text to talk about their questions, you might want to repeat this week using an alternative book before moving on to Unit 4. Alternative books are listed in the Week 3 Overview. Be aware that students will have more opportunities to practice "Stop and Ask Questions" in the coming units.

Notes:

Analyzing Text Structure—

Fiction and Narrative Nonfiction

Observe the students and ask yourself:	All or most students	About half of the students	Only a few students
▶ *Do the students use evidence from the text to make predictions and support their thinking?*			

What to do now:

▶ If *all or most students* are able to use evidence from the text to make predictions and support their thinking, proceed with Day 4.

▶ If *about half the students* are able to use evidence from the text to make predictions and support their thinking, proceed with Day 4. There will be additional opportunities for the students to practice this in Week 2. You may wish to check in with students who are having difficulty during IDR.

▶ If *only a few students* are able to use evidence from the text to make predictions and support their thinking, you might want to repeat Day 3 of this week using an alternative book before moving on to Day 4. Alternative books are listed in the Week 1 Overview.

Notes:

Analyzing Text Structure—
Fiction and Narrative Nonfiction

Observe the students and ask yourself:	All or most students	About half of the students	Only a few students
▸ Do the students notice the conflicts that characters are facing in their stories?			
▸ Are students who are at the end of a story able to describe how a character changes?			

What to do now:

▸ If **all or most students** are able to describe characters' conflicts and change, proceed with Week 3.

▸ If **about half the students** or **only a few students** are able to describe characters' conflicts and change, continue with Week 3 and closely monitor and support students who are having difficulty. Confer with them during IDR and ask them questions such as:

   Q *What problems are the characters in your story facing?*

   Q *How do you think those characters [changed/might change] in the story?*

Notes:

Analyzing Text Structure—

Fiction and Narrative Nonfiction

Observe the students and ask yourself:	All or most students	About half of the students	Only a few students
▶ *Are the students using their questions to discuss the story?*			
▶ *Are the students giving evidence from the text to explain their thinking?*			

What to do now:

▶ If *all or most students* are using questioning and evidence from the text to discuss the story, proceed with Week 4.

▶ If *about half the students* are using questioning and evidence from the text to discuss the story, proceed with Week 4 and monitor students who are having difficulty with questioning during IDR.

▶ If *only a few students* are using questioning and evidence from the text to discuss the story, consider repeating this week using an alternative book before moving on to Week 4. Alternative books are listed in the Week 3 Overview.

Notes:

Analyzing Text Structure—
Fiction and Narrative Nonfiction

Observe the students and ask yourself:	All or most students	About half of the students	Only a few students
▶ *Are the students using their questions to talk about their reading?*			
▶ *Are they referring to the text to discuss their questions?*			

What to do now:

▶ If **all or most students** are using questioning to understand and discuss their independent reading, proceed with Unit 5.

▶ If **about half the students** or **only a few students** are using questioning to understand and discuss their independent reading, repeat this week using an alternative book before moving on to Unit 5. Alternative books are listed in the Weeks 3 and 4 Overviews. Closely monitor and support students who are having difficulty by asking them questions during IDR and partner work, for example:

    Q *What are you wondering about at this point in your reading?*

    Q *What is a question you could ask at this point in the reading?*

    Q *What question got you and your partner talking about the book?*

Notes:

Making Inferences—Fiction and Poetry

Observe the students and ask yourself:	All or most students	About half of the students	Only a few students
▸ Are the students underlining passages that give clues that it is storming?			
▸ Are they able to explain how a passage tells them that it's storming?			

What to do now:

▸ If **all or most students** are identifying clues that it is storming, proceed with Independent Strategy Practice on Day 3.

▸ If **about half the students** or **only a few students** are identifying clues that it is storming, you might want to repeat Days 1 and 2 of this week using an alternative book before moving on to Day 3. Alternative books are listed in the Week 1 Overview.

Notes:

Making Inferences—Fiction and Poetry

Observe the students and ask yourself:	All or most students	About half of the students	Only a few students
▶ Are the students able to identify lines in the poem that require an inference?			
▶ Are they able to make an appropriate inference for those lines?			

What to do now:

▶ If **all or most students** are able to make inferences, proceed with Independent Strategy Practice on Day 4.

▶ If **about half the students** are able to make inferences, proceed with Day 4, but plan to monitor the students who are having difficulty with inferences during IDR by asking them questions such as:

    Q *What is one thing that you know based on what you read today?*

    Q *Did the book tell you that directly, or did you figure it out from clues? What clues?*

▶ If **only a few students** are able to make inferences, consider repeating Days 1, 2, and 3 of this week using an alternative poem before moving on to Day 4. Alternative poems are listed in the Week 2 Overview.

Notes:

Making Inferences—Fiction and Poetry

Observe the students and ask yourself:	All or most students	About half of the students	Only a few students
▸ Are the students able to describe what happens in the poem?			
▸ Are their visualizations connected to the text?			
▸ Are they recognizing clues in the poem that help them make inferences?			

What to do now:

▸ If **all or most students** are able to make inferences and visualize what is happening in the poem, proceed with Independent Strategy Practice on Day 3.

▸ If **about half the students** or **only a few students** are able to make inferences and visualize what is happening in the poem, consider repeating Days 1 and 2 of this week using an alternative poem before moving on to Day 3. Alternative poems are listed in the Week 3 Overview.

Notes:

Making Inferences—Fiction and Narrative Nonfiction

Observe the students and ask yourself:	All or most students	About half of the students	Only a few students
▶ *Are the students underlining passages that give clues about the reasons for Amelia's actions?*			
▶ *Do their inferences about Amelia's actions make sense?*			

What to do now:

▶ If ***all or most students*** are able to identify clues about Amelia's actions that make sense, proceed with Independent Strategy Practice on Day 4.

▶ If ***about half the students*** are able to identify clues about Amelia's actions that make sense, proceed with Day 4, but plan to check in with students who are having difficulty making inferences during IDR.

▶ If ***only a few students*** are able to identify clues about Amelia's actions that make sense, repeat Days 1, 2, and 3 of this week using an alternative book before moving on to Day 4. Alternative books are listed in the Week 1 Overview.

Notes:

Making Inferences—Fiction and Narrative Nonfiction

Observe the students and ask yourself:	All or most students	About half of the students	Only a few students
▶ Are the students underlining passages that give clues about Peppe's character?			
▶ Do their inferences about Peppe make sense?			

What to do now:

▶ If **all or most students** are able to identify clues about Peppe's character that make sense, proceed with Independent Strategy Practice on Day 4.

▶ If **about half the students** or **only a few students** are able to identify clues about Peppe's character that make sense, proceed with Day 4, but plan to check in with students who are having difficulty during IDR. You might have these students tell you about what they just read, then follow up with questions such as:

     Q *What did you read about today?*

     Q *What is one thing you know about a character in your book? What clues told you that?*

Notes:

Making Inferences—Fiction and Narrative Nonfiction

Observe the students and ask yourself:	All or most students	About half of the students	Only a few students
▸ *Are the students identifying clues about why immigrants were examined and questioned at Ellis Island?*			

What to do now:

▸ If **all or most students** are able to identify clues about why immigrants were examined and questioned at Ellis Island, proceed with Independent Strategy Practice on Day 4.

▸ If **about half the students** or **only a few students** are able to identify clues about why immigrants were examined and questioned at Ellis Island, repeat Days 1, 2, and 3 of this week using an alternative book before moving on to Day 4. Alternative books are listed in the Week 3 Overview.

Notes:

Making Inferences—Fiction and Narrative Nonfiction

Observe the students and ask yourself:	All or most students	About half of the students	Only a few students
▶ *Are the students underlining sentences that give clues about why John Brown called Harriet "General Tubman"?*			
▶ *Can they support their inferences using evidence from the text?*			

What to do now:

▶ If *all or most students* are able to identify clues about why John Brown called Harriet "General Tubman," proceed with Unit 7.

▶ If *about half the students* or *only a few students* are able to identify clues about why John Brown called Harriet "General Tubman," repeat this week using an alternative book before moving on to Unit 7. Alternative books are listed in the Week 4 Overview.

Closely monitor the students who are having difficulty identifying simple causal relationships during IDR by asking them questions such as:

Q *What is a* why *question you can ask about the part of the book you are reading right now?*

Q *Do you have any information so far that might help you answer that* why *question? If so, what information?*

Notes:

Analyzing Text Structure—Expository Nonfiction

Observe the students and ask yourself:	All or most students	About half of the students	Only a few students
▶ Do the students understand the article?			
▶ Are they able to identify examples that support the point of view expressed in the article?			

What to do now:

▶ If **all or most students** are able to identify examples that support the point of view expressed, proceed with Week 2.

▶ If **about half the students** or **only a few students** are able to identify examples that support the point of view expressed in the article, repeat this week using alternative articles from the alternative resources before moving on to Week 2. Alternative resources are listed on the Week 1 Overview.

Notes:

Analyzing Text Structure—Expository Nonfiction

Observe the students and ask yourself:	All or most students	About half of the students	Only a few students
▶ Are the students able to read and use the functional text?			
▶ Are students taking responsibility for their own learning?			

What to do now:

▶ If **all or most students** are able to read and use the functional text, proceed with Day 3.

▶ If **about half the students** or **only a few students** are able to read and use the functional text, repeat Days 1 and 2 using a functional text from the alternative resources before moving on to Day 3. Alternative resources are listed in the Week 2 Overview.

Notes:

Analyzing Text Structure—Expository Nonfiction

Observe the students and ask yourself:	All or most students	About half of the students	Only a few students
▶ Are the students able to identify what they've learned from the book?			
▶ Are they contributing their thinking to the group?			
▶ Are they using prompts to extend their conversations?			

What to do now:

▶ If **all or most students** are identifying what they've learned from the book, contributing their thinking to the group, and using prompts to extend their conversations, proceed with Week 4.

▶ If **about half the students** or **only a few students** are identifying what they've learned from the book, contributing their thinking to the group, and using prompts to extend their conversations, repeat all or part of this week using an alternative book before moving on to Week 4. Alternative books are listed in the Week 3 Overview.

Notes:

✎ **Analyzing Text Structure**—Expository Nonfiction

Observe the students and ask yourself:	All or most students	About half of the students	Only a few students
▶ *Do the students notice how their texts are organized?*			
▶ *Do they recognize chronological and compare and contrast relationships in their reading?*			

What to do now:

▶ If ***all or most students*** are able to identify how their texts are organized, proceed with Day 4.

▶ If ***about half the students*** or ***only a few students*** are able to identify how their texts are organized, repeat Days 1 and 2 of this week using an alternative text, then repeat Day 3 before moving on to Day 4. Alternative texts are listed in the Week 4 Overview.

Notes:

Determining Important Ideas and Summarizing—Narrative Nonfiction

Observe the students and ask yourself:	All or most students	About half of the students	Only a few students
▸ Are the students able to identify an important idea from the story?			
▸ Are they able to identify a supporting idea?			
▸ Is there evidence that they see the difference between important and supporting ideas in the passage?			

What to do now:

▸ If **all or most students** are able to identify and distinguish between important and supporting ideas, proceed with Week 2.

▸ If **about half the students** are able to identify and distinguish between important and supporting ideas, proceed with Week 2 and continue to closely observe the students who are not identifying and distinguishing these ideas. Many students will need repeated experiences to learn this complex skill.

▸ If **only a few students** are able to identify and distinguish between important and supporting ideas, repeat this week's lessons using an alternative book before moving on to Week 2. Alternative books are listed in the Week 1 Overview.

Notes:

Determining Important Ideas and Summarizing—Narrative Nonfiction

Observe the students and ask yourself:	All or most students	About half of the students	Only a few students
▸ Are the students making reasonable distinctions between important and supporting information?			
▸ Are they supporting their thinking by referring to the story?			

What to do now:

▸ If **all or most students** are making reasonable distinctions between important and supporting information and are referring to the text to support their thinking, proceed with Week 3.

▸ If **about half the students** or **only a few students** are making reasonable distinctions between important and supporting ideas or referring to the text to support their thinking, repeat this week's lessons using an alternative book before moving on to Week 3. Alternative books are listed in the Week 2 Overview.

Notes:

Determining Important Ideas and Summarizing—Narrative Nonfiction

Observe the students and ask yourself:	All or most students	About half of the students	Only a few students
▸ Are the students able to identify important information in the text?			
▸ Are they referring to the text to support their thinking?			

What to do now:

▸ If **all or most students** are identifying important information and referring to the text to support their thinking, proceed with Day 4.

▸ If **about half the students** or **only a few students** are identifying important information and referring to the text to support their thinking, continue with the guided summarization lesson on Day 4, but plan to model writing the entire summary with the class. Then plan to repeat this week's lesson using an alternative book before moving on to Week 4. Alternative books are listed in the Week 3 Overview.

Notes:

Determining Important Ideas and Summarizing—Narrative Nonfiction

Observe the students and ask yourself:	All or most students	About half of the students	Only a few students
▶ Are the students able to identify important ideas in each section?			
▶ Can they summarize the information in a few sentences?			

What to do now:

▶ If **all or most students** are able to identify important ideas in each section and summarize the information in a few sentences, proceed with Week 5.

▶ If **about half the students** or **only a few students** are able to identify important ideas in each section and summarize the information in a few sentences, bring the class together and summarize the remaining sections of the excerpt together, as you did in Steps 2 and 3 of today's lesson. Then plan to repeat the week using an alternative book before continuing with Week 5. Alternative books are listed in the Week 4 Overview.

Notes:

Determining Important Ideas and Summarizing—Narrative Nonfiction

Observe the students and ask yourself:	All or most students	About half of the students	Only a few students
▶ Do the students' summaries successfully communicate what their texts are about?			
▶ Is there evidence in the partners' feedback that they understand something about the texts being summarized?			
▶ Are the students revising or adding to their summaries based on the feedback?			

What to do now:

▶ If **all or most students** are writing summaries that successfully communicate what their texts are about, continue with the Class Meeting on Day 4 and proceed with Unit 9.

▶ If **about half the students** are writing summaries that successfully communicate what their texts are about, collect the unsuccessful summaries, read them, and give feedback to the students. Have the students write second drafts based on your feedback (see the Teacher Note on Day 3, Step 3 of the lesson). Then continue with Unit 9.

▶ If **only a few students** are writing summaries that successfully communicate what their texts are about, do the Extension activity at the end of Week 4, Day 4. If you have already done the Extension once with the students' Rosa Parks summaries, do it again using photocopies of the students' own summaries from Week 5. Make sure to copy their summaries without their names. After analyzing the summaries in the Extension activity, have the students select another short text to summarize, and repeat Days 1, 2, and 3 of Week 5.

Notes:

Individual
Comprehension
Assessment

Recognizing Text Features—Expository Nonfiction

The strategy-specific assessment helps you assess whether a student is able to use a strategy when prompted in a lesson. The ongoing comprehension assessment helps you assess his overall comprehension during IDR conferences. Be aware that a student may or may not use any particular strategy to make sense of his independent reading. The goal over time is for the students to be able to use appropriate strategies as needed to help them make sense of the texts they read independently.

Part 1: Strategy-specific Assessment

Review and consider for each student:

▸ Student work in Unit 2, including:
  • *Student Response Book*, pages 3–15
  • *Student Book*, IDR Journal entries

As you analyze each student's work, ask yourself:

▸ *Does the student recognize and use text features to make sense of expository text?*

3 *Yes, most* of the student's work shows that he recognizes and uses text features to make sense of expository text.

2 *Some* of the student's work shows that he recognizes and uses text features to make sense of expository text.

1 *No, hardly any* of the student's work shows that he recognizes and uses text features to make sense of expository text.

Part 2: Ongoing IDR Assessment

Review and consider for each student:

▸ Your observations and impressions during IDR conferences in Unit 2.

Ask yourself:

▸ *Does this student show evidence that he is actively engaging with and making sense of text?*

3 *Yes, most* of my observations and impressions show evidence that he is actively engaging with and making sense of text.

2 *Some* of my observations and impressions show evidence that he is actively engaging with and making sense of text.

1 *No, hardly any* of my observations and impressions show evidence that he is actively engaging with and making sense of text.

Record your two assessment scores for each student on the ICA Class Record Sheet on page 48. Note that these scores denote the level of evidence *across* a student's work, rather than on any particular piece of work. Use the examples on the facing page as a benchmark for your assessments.

Examples for a student who would score 3 on both assessments:

Part 1: Strategy-specific Assessment

▸ Recognizes text features and has a sense of the information they contribute to the text.

Think, Pair, Write
About Text Features

Name: *Nathan*

What information about Italian American immigrants can you find in the text features? Share your thinking with your partner. Then write the things you found out.

Italian immigrants have been coming to the U.S. for more than 180 years.

In 1900, many Italians lived on Mulberry Street in New York.

In the picture, Mulberry Street looks very crowded.

Some people left Italy because of an earthquake.

World War I stopped people from leaving Italy.

Some people dreamed of coming to America because they missed their families.

14 | Making Meaning®   Unit 2 ▸ Week 3 ▸ Day 2

Part 2: Ongoing IDR Assessment

▸ Describes what is happening in narrative texts he reads.

▸ Explains what he is learning from nonfiction or expository texts he reads.

▸ Notices when comprehension breaks down and stops to reread or question.

Commentary

The goal is for students to naturally recognize and use text features to think about and make sense of expository text. Students will be at different levels in learning to use this strategy. This is to be expected as students' sense-making develops over time with repeated reading experiences.

Continue to help the students practice by prompting them to demonstrate their use of this strategy in their independent reading.

Questioning—Expository Nonfiction

The strategy-specific assessment helps you assess whether a student is able to use a strategy when prompted in a lesson. The ongoing comprehension assessment helps you assess her overall comprehension during IDR conferences. Be aware that a student may or may not use any particular strategy to make sense of her independent reading. The goal over time is for the students to be able to use appropriate strategies as needed to help them make sense of the texts they read independently.

Part 1: Strategy-specific Assessment

Review and consider for each student:

▶ Student work in Unit 3, including:
  • *Student Response Book*, pages 16–18
  • *Student Response Book*, IDR Journal entries

As you analyze each student's work, ask yourself:

▶ *Does the student use questioning to make sense of expository text?*

3 *Yes, most* of the student's work shows that she uses questioning to make sense of expository text.

2 *Some* of the student's work shows that she uses questioning to make sense of expository text.

1 *No, hardly any* of the student's work shows that she uses questioning to make sense of expository text.

Part 2: Ongoing IDR Assessment

Review and consider for each student:

▶ Your observations and impressions during IDR conferences in Unit 3.

Ask yourself:

▶ *Does this student show evidence that she is actively engaging with and making sense of text?*

3 *Yes, most* of my observations and impressions show evidence that she is actively engaging with and making sense of text.

2 *Some* of my observations and impressions show evidence that she is actively engaging with and making sense of text.

1 *No, hardly any* of my observations and impressions show evidence that she is actively engaging with and making sense of text.

Record your two assessment scores for each student on the ICA Class Record Sheet on page 48. Note that these scores denote the level of evidence *across* a student's work, rather than on any particular piece of work. Use the examples on the facing page as a benchmark for your assessments.

Examples for a student who would score 3 on both assessments:

Part 1: Strategy-specific Assessment

▶ Uses questioning to help her think about and discuss a text.

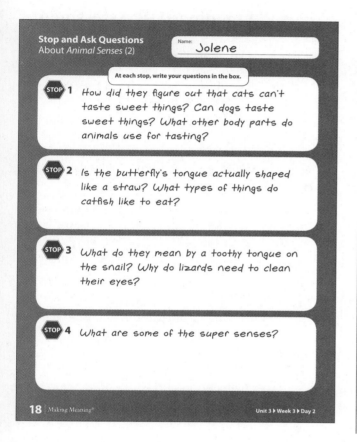

Stop and Ask Questions
About *Animal Senses* (2)

Name: Jolene

At each stop, write your questions in the box.

STOP 1 How did they figure out that cats can't taste sweet things? Can dogs taste sweet things? What other body parts do animals use for tasting?

STOP 2 Is the butterfly's tongue actually shaped like a straw? What types of things do catfish like to eat?

STOP 3 What do they mean by a toothy tongue on the snail? Why do lizards need to clean their eyes?

STOP 4 What are some of the super senses?

18 Making Meaning®   Unit 3 ▶ Week 3 ▶ Day 2

Part 2: Ongoing IDR Assessment

▶ Describes what is happening in narrative texts she reads.

▶ Explains what she is learning from nonfiction or expository texts she reads.

▶ Notices when comprehension breaks down and stops to reread or question.

Commentary

The goal is for the students to use questioning to make sense of expository texts. Students will be at different levels in learning to use this strategy. This is to be expected as students' sense-making develops over time with repeated reading experiences.

Continue to help the students practice by prompting them to demonstrate their use of this strategy in their independent reading.

Analyzing Text Structure—Fiction and Narrative Nonfiction

The strategy-specific assessment helps you assess whether a student is able to use a strategy when prompted in a lesson. The ongoing comprehension assessment helps you assess his overall comprehension during IDR conferences. Be aware that a student may or may not use any particular strategy to make sense of his independent reading. The goal over time is for the students to be able to use appropriate strategies as needed to help them make sense of the texts they read independently.

Part 1: Strategy-specific Assessment

Review and consider for each student:

▶ Student work in Unit 4, including:
  • *Student Response Book*, pages 19–22
  • *Student Response Book*, IDR Journal entries

As you analyze each student's work, ask yourself:

▶ *Does the student use questioning to make sense of narrative texts?*

3 *Yes, most* of the student's work shows evidence of using questioning to make sense of narrative text.

2 *Some* of the student's work shows evidence of using questioning to make sense of narrative text.

1 *No, hardly any* of the student's work shows evidence of using questioning to make sense of narrative text.

Part 2: Ongoing IDR Assessment

Review and consider for each student:

▶ Your IDR conference notes from Unit 4.

As you analyze each student's "IDR Conference Notes," ask yourself:

▶ *Do the conference notes for this student show evidence that he is actively engaging with and making sense of text?*

3 *Yes, most* of the notes show evidence that he is actively engaging with and making sense of text.

2 *Some* of the notes show evidence that he is actively engaging with and making sense of text.

1 *No, hardly any* of the notes show evidence that he is actively engaging with and making sense of text.

Record your two assessment scores for each student on the ICA Class Record Sheet on page 48. Note that these scores denote the level of evidence *across* a student's work, rather than on any particular piece of work. Use the examples on the facing page as a benchmark for your assessments.

Examples for a student who would score 3 on both assessments:

Part 1: Strategy-specific Assessment

▶ Generates relevant questions for a variety of texts.

▶ Uses his questions to discuss a text.

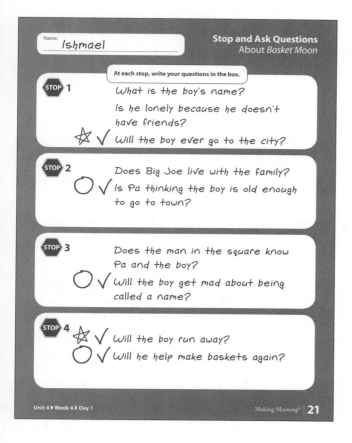

Part 2: Ongoing IDR Assessment

▶ Describes what is happening in narrative texts he reads.

▶ Explains what he is learning from nonfiction or expository texts he reads.

▶ Notices when comprehension breaks down and stops to reread or question.

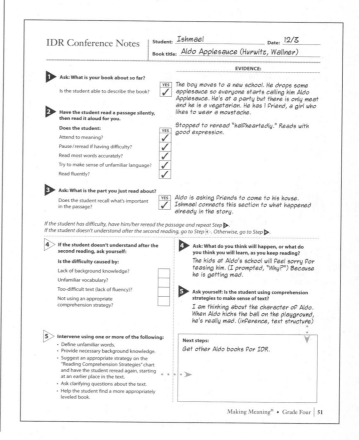

Commentary

At this point in the program, some students may be able to use questioning only when prompted. This is to be expected. With time and practice, the students will learn to use questioning spontaneously and as needed to make sense of their independent reading. During IDR conferences, continue to encourage the students to talk about questions that come to mind and to use their questions to help them think about the text.

Making Inferences—Fiction and Poetry

The strategy-specific assessment helps you assess whether a student is able to use a strategy when prompted in a lesson. The ongoing comprehension assessment helps you assess her overall comprehension during IDR conferences. Be aware that a student may or may not use any particular strategy to make sense of her independent reading. The goal over time is for the students to be able to use appropriate strategies as needed to help them make sense of the texts they read independently.

Part 1: Strategy-specific Assessment

Review and consider for each student:

▸ Student work in Unit 5, including:
  • *Student Response Book*, pages 23–32
  • *Student Response Book*, IDR Journal entries

As you analyze each student's work, ask yourself:

▸ *Does the student make inferences to understand a variety of texts, including poems?*

3 *Yes, most* of the student's work shows evidence of making inferences to understand text.

2 *Some* of the student's work shows evidence of making inferences to understand text.

1 *No, hardly any* of the student's work shows evidence of making inferences to understand text.

Part 2: Ongoing IDR Assessment

Review and consider for each student:

▸ Your IDR conference notes from Unit 5.

As you analyze each student's "IDR Conference Notes," ask yourself:

▸ *Do the conference notes for this student show evidence that she is actively engaging with and making sense of text?*

3 *Yes, most* of the notes show evidence that she is actively engaging with and making sense of text.

2 *Some* of the notes show evidence that she is actively engaging with and making sense of text.

1 *No, hardly any* of the notes show evidence that she is actively engaging with and making sense of text.

Record your two assessment scores for each student on the ICA Class Record Sheet on page 48. Note that these scores denote the level of evidence *across* a student's work, rather than on any particular piece of work. Use the examples on the facing page as a benchmark for your assessments.

Examples for a student who would score 3 on both assessments:

Part 1: Strategy-specific Assessment

▶ Describes what is happening in a variety of texts, including poems.

▶ Recognizes clues in poems and texts that can be used to make inferences.

▶ Describes inferences based on clues.

Part 2: Ongoing IDR Assessment

▶ Describes what is happening in narrative texts she reads.

▶ Explains what she is learning from nonfiction or expository texts she reads.

▶ Notices when comprehension breaks down and stops to reread or question.

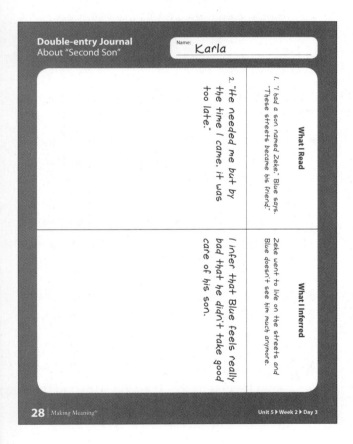

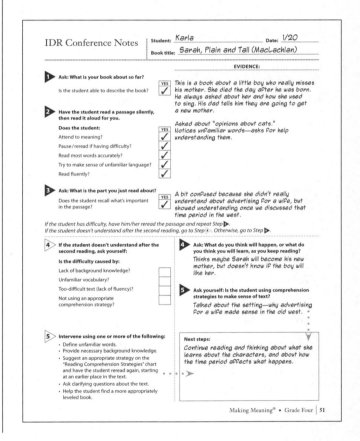

Commentary

At this point in the program, some students may be aware of their inferences only when prompted. During IDR conferences, continue to encourage these students to talk about what they know from their reading and the clues that helped them understand these things. As with all the strategies, the goal over time is for the students to be able to make inferences naturally and as appropriate as they read independently.

Making Inferences—Fiction and Narrative Nonfiction

The strategy-specific assessment helps you assess whether a student is able to use a strategy when prompted in a lesson. The ongoing comprehension assessment helps you assess his overall comprehension during IDR conferences. Be aware that a student may or may not use any particular strategy to make sense of his independent reading. The goal over time is for the students to be able to use appropriate strategies as needed to help them make sense of the texts they read independently.

Part 1: Strategy-specific Assessment

Review and consider for each student:

▸ Student work in Unit 6, including:
  • *Student Response Book*, pages 33–37
  • *Student Response Book*, IDR Journal entries

As you analyze each student's work, ask yourself:

▸ *Does the student identify simple causes in texts by answering* why *questions?*

3 *Yes, most* of the student's work shows that he identifies simple causes in texts by answering *why* questions.

2 *Some* of the student's work shows that he identifies simple causes in texts by answering *why* questions.

1 *No, hardly any* of the student's work shows that he identifies simple causes in texts by answering *why* questions.

Part 2: Ongoing IDR Assessment

Review and consider for each student:

▸ Your IDR conference notes from Unit 6.

As you analyze each student's "IDR Conference Notes," ask yourself:

▸ *Do the conference notes for this student show evidence that he is actively engaging with and making sense of text?*

3 *Yes, most* of the notes show evidence that he is actively engaging with and making sense of text.

2 *Some* of the notes show evidence that he is actively engaging with and making sense of text.

1 *No, hardly any* of the notes show evidence that he is actively engaging with and making sense of text.

Record your two assessment scores for each student on the ICA Class Record Sheet on page 48. Note that these scores denote the level of evidence *across* a student's work, rather than on any particular piece of work. Use the examples on the facing page as a benchmark for your assessments.

Examples for a student who would score 3 on both assessments:

Part 1: Strategy-specific Assessment

▶ Uses clues in text to answer *why* questions about a text.

▶ Uses evidence from the text to support answers to *why* questions.

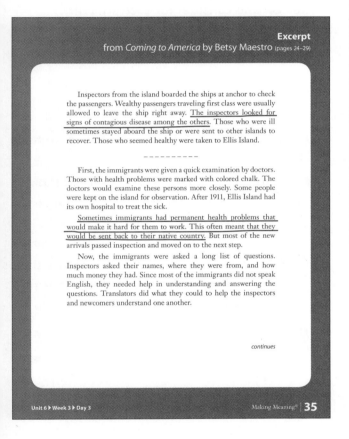

Part 2: Ongoing IDR Assessment

▶ Describes what is happening in narrative texts he reads.

▶ Explains what he is learning from nonfiction or expository texts he reads.

▶ Notices when comprehension breaks down and stops to reread or question.

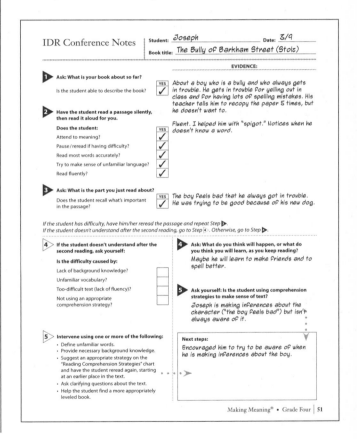

Commentary

At this point in the program, it is likely that many students will be able to identify causes in texts only when asked specific *why* questions. This is to be expected. During IDR conferences, continue to encourage the students to talk about the *why* questions that come to mind as they read. As with all the strategies, the goal over time is for the students to be able to think about causal relationships as appropriate to help them make sense of the texts they read independently. They will explore cause and effect relationships in more depth in *Making Meaning* grades 5 and 6.

Analyzing Text Structure—Expository Nonfiction

The strategy-specific assessment helps you assess whether a student is able to use a strategy when prompted in a lesson. The ongoing comprehension assessment helps you assess her overall comprehension during IDR conferences. Be aware that a student may or may not use any particular strategy to make sense of her independent reading. The goal over time is for the students to be able to use appropriate strategies as needed to help them make sense of the texts they read independently.

Part 1: Strategy-specific Assessment

Review and consider for each student:

▶ Student work in Unit 7, including:
  • Your observations of the students during partner, group, and class discussions
  • *Student Response Book*, IDR Journal entries

As you analyze each student's work and performance, ask yourself:

▶ *Does the student recognize the different ways expository text is organized?*

3 *Yes, most* of the student's work and performance shows that she recognizes the different ways expository text is organized.

2 *Some* of the student's work and performance shows that she recognizes the different ways expository text is organized.

1 *No, hardly any* of the student's work and performance shows that she recognizes the different ways expository text is organized.

Part 2: Ongoing IDR Assessment

Review and consider for each student:

▶ Your IDR conference notes from Unit 7.

As you analyze each student's "IDR Conference Notes," ask yourself:

▶ *Do the conference notes for this student show evidence that she is actively engaging with and making sense of text?*

3 *Yes, most* of the notes show evidence that she is actively engaging with and making sense of text.

2 *Some* of the notes show evidence that she is actively engaging with and making sense of text.

1 *No, hardly any* of the notes show evidence that she is actively engaging with and making sense of text.

Record your two assessment scores for each student on the ICA Class Record Sheet on page 48. Note that these scores denote the level of evidence *across* a student's work, rather than on any particular piece of work. Use the examples on the facing page as a benchmark for your assessments.

Examples for a student who would score 3 on both assessments:

Part 1: Strategy-specific Assessment

▶ Recognizes the different ways expository text is organized.

▶ Identifies passages in expository texts that show the different text structures.

Part 2: Ongoing IDR Assessment

▶ Describes what is happening in narrative texts she reads.

▶ Explains what she is learning from nonfiction or expository texts she reads.

▶ Notices when comprehension breaks down and stops to reread or question.

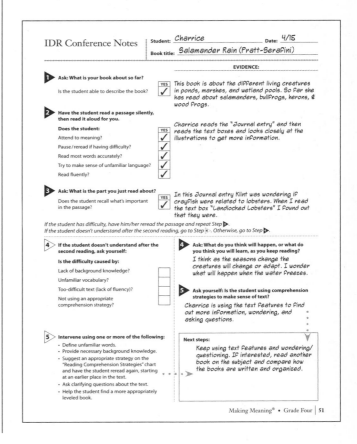

Commentary

Identifying chronological and compare and contrast relationships may be challenging and abstract for students. Many students may be able to identify these only after seeing several examples. The ability to identify these relationships develops with practice over time. During IDR conferences, continue to encourage the students to talk about the relationships they notice in expository text. This unit lays the foundation for more in-depth work analyzing expository text in later grades.

Determining Important Ideas and Summarizing—
Narrative Nonfiction

The strategy-specific assessment helps you assess whether a student is able to use a strategy when prompted in a lesson. The ongoing comprehension assessment helps you assess his overall comprehension during IDR conferences. Be aware that a student may or may not use any particular strategy to make sense of his independent reading. The goal over time is for the students to be able to use appropriate strategies as needed to help them make sense of the texts they read independently.

Part 1: Strategy-specific Assessment	Part 2: Ongoing IDR Assessment
Review and consider for each student:	**Review and consider for each student:**
▸ Student work in Unit 8, including: • *Student Response Book*, pages 56–64 • Written summary of *A Picture Book of Rosa Parks* from Weeks 4 and 5 • *Student Response Book*, IDR Journal entries	▸ Your IDR conference notes from Unit 8.
As you analyze each student's work, ask yourself:	**As you analyze each student's "IDR Conference Notes," ask yourself:**
▸ *Does the student identify important and supporting information and summarize from the important information?*	▸ *Do the conference notes for this student show evidence that he is actively engaging with and making sense of text?*
3 *Yes, most* of the student's work shows that that he identifies important and supporting information and summarizes.	**3** *Yes, most* of the notes show evidence that he is actively engaging with and making sense of text.
2 *Some* of the student's work shows that he identifies important and supporting information and summarizes.	**2** *Some* of the notes show evidence that he is actively engaging with and making sense of text.
1 *No, hardly any* of the student's work shows that he identifies important and supporting information and summarizes.	**1** *No, hardly any* of the notes show evidence that he is actively engaging with and making sense of text.

Record your two assessment scores for each student on the ICA Class Record Sheet on page 48. Note that these scores denote the level of evidence *across* a student's work, rather than on any particular piece of work. Use the examples on the facing page as a benchmark for your assessments.

Examples for a student who would score 3 on both assessments:

Part 1: Strategy-specific Assessment

▶ Distinguishes between important and supporting ideas in texts.

▶ Refers to the texts to explain how information supports important ideas.

▶ Uses important ideas to summarize texts.

Aleksei

Summary of A Picture Book of Rosa Parks

This section of the story tells about how Rosa took a stand to change unfair laws. Rosa decided it was unfair to have to go to the back of the bus, since she had paid the same amount as the white passengers. She refused to move and was arrested. Other African Americans also felt that the law was unfair, and said they would not ride the buses until the law was changed. Finally, the Supreme Court decided that the law was wrong. Rosa Parks was a brave person who helped make life better for African Americans.

Part 2: Ongoing IDR Assessment

▶ Describes what is happening in narrative texts he reads.

▶ Explains what he is learning from nonfiction or expository texts he reads.

▶ Notices when comprehension breaks down and stops to reread or question.

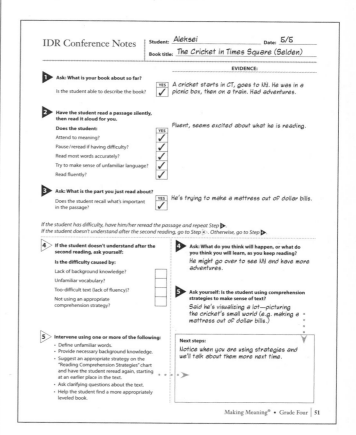

Commentary

In grade 4, the students explore the notion that ideas in text have different levels of significance, and that identifying the most important ideas can help them summarize and communicate with others about a text. Distinguishing between important and supporting ideas is a complex skill. At the end of this unit, some of your students will continue to need support in identifying important ideas and summarizing. The students will continue to explore these concepts in *Making Meaning* grades 5 and 6.

Student Names	UNIT 2	UNIT 3	UNIT 4	UNIT 5	UNIT 6	UNIT 7	UNIT 8

Blackline Masters

Resource Sheet for IDR Conferences

General questions you can ask to probe student thinking:

▶ *Why did you choose this book?*

▶ *Why do you like/dislike this book?*

▶ *What kinds of books do you want to read?*

Genre-specific questions you can ask:

Fiction

▶ *What is this story about?*

▶ *What has happened so far?*

▶ *What do you know about the character(s)?*

▶ *What part have you found interesting or surprising? Why?*

▶ *What are you wondering about?*

▶ *What do you visualize (see/hear/feel) as you read these words?*

▶ *What do you think will happen next?*

Nonfiction/Expository

▶ *What is this [book/article] about?*

▶ *(Read the information on the back cover.) What have you found out about that so far?*

▶ *(Look at the table of contents.) What do you think you will find out about _____ in this book?*

▶ *What have you learned from reading this article?*

▶ *What's something interesting you've read so far?*

▶ *What are you wondering about?*

▶ *What do you expect to learn about as you continue to read?*

▶ *What information does this [diagram/table/graph/other text feature] give you?*

Poetry

▶ *What is this poem about?*

▶ *What do you visualize (see/hear/feel) as you read these words?*

▶ *What do you think the poet means by _____ ?*

IDR Conference Notes

Student: _____ **Date:** _____

Book title: _____

EVIDENCE: _____

1 ▶ **Ask: What is your book about so far?**

Is the student able to describe the book? | YES ☐

2 ▶ **Have the student read a passage silently, then read it aloud for you.**

Does the student: | YES

Attend to meaning? ☐

Pause/reread if having difficulty? ☐

Read most words accurately? ☐

Try to make sense of unfamiliar language? ☐

Read fluently? ☐

3 ▶ **Ask: What is the part you just read about?**

Does the student recall what's important in the passage? | YES ☐

If the student has difficulty, have him/her reread the passage and repeat Step ▶3.
If the student doesn't understand after the second reading, go to Step ▷4. Otherwise, go to Step ▶4.

- -

4 ▷ **If the student doesn't understand after the second reading, ask yourself:**

Is the difficulty caused by:

Lack of background knowledge? ☐

Unfamiliar vocabulary? ☐

Too-difficult text (lack of fluency)? ☐

Not using an appropriate comprehension strategy? ☐

5 ▷ **Intervene using one or more of the following:**

- Define unfamiliar words.
- Provide necessary background knowledge.
- Suggest an appropriate strategy on the "Reading Comprehension Strategies" chart and have the student reread again, starting at an earlier place in the text.
- Ask clarifying questions about the text.
- Help the student find a more appropriately leveled book.

4 ▶ **Ask: What do you think will happen, or what do you think you will learn, as you keep reading?**

5 ▶ **Ask yourself: Is the student using comprehension strategies to make sense of text?**

Next steps:

Making Meaning®
SECOND EDITION

Reorder Information

Kindergarten

Complete Classroom Package　　　　**MM2-CPK**

Contents: Teacher's Manual, Orientation Handbook and DVDs, and 27 trade books

Available separately:

Classroom materials without trade books	MM2-TPK
Teacher's Manual	MM2-TMK
Trade book set (27 books)	MM2-TBSK

Grade 1

Complete Classroom Package　　　　**MM2-CP1**

Contents: Teacher's Manual, Orientation Handbook and DVDs, Assessment Resource Book, and 28 trade books

Available separately:

Classroom materials without trade books	MM2-TP1
Teacher's Manual	MM2-TM1
Assessment Resource Book	MM2-AB1
Trade book set (28 books)	MM2-TBS1

Grade 2

Complete Classroom Package　　　　**MM2-CP2**

Contents: Teacher's Manual, Orientation Handbook and DVDs, class set (25 Student Response Books, Assessment Resource Book), and 29 trade books

Available separately:

Classroom materials without trade books	MM2-TP2
Teacher's Manual	MM2-TM2
Replacement class set	MM2-RCS2
CD-ROM Grade 2 Reproducible Materials	MM2-CDR2
Trade book set (29 books)	MM2-TBS2

Grade 3

Complete Classroom Package　　　　**MM2-CP3**

Contents: Teacher's Manual (2 volumes), Orientation Handbook and DVDs, class set (25 Student Response Books, Assessment Resource Book), and 26 trade books

Available separately:

Classroom materials without trade books	MM2-TP3
Teacher's Manual, vol. 1	MM2-TM3-V1
Teacher's Manual, vol. 2	MM2-TM3-V2
Replacement class set	MM2-RCS3
CD-ROM Grade 3 Reproducible Materials	MM2-CDR3
Trade book set (26 books)	MM2-TBS3

Grade 4

Complete Classroom Package　　　　**MM2-CP4**

Contents: Teacher's Manual (2 volumes), Orientation Handbook and DVDs, class set (30 Student Response Books, Assessment Resource Book), and 24 trade books

Available separately:

Classroom materials without trade books	MM2-TP4
Teacher's Manual, vol. 1	MM2-TM4-V1
Teacher's Manual, vol. 2	MM2-TM4-V2
Replacement class set	MM2-RCS4
CD-ROM Grade 4 Reproducible Materials	MM2-CDR4
Trade book set (24 books)	MM2-TBS4

Grade 5

Complete Classroom Package　　　　**MM2-CP5**

Contents: Teacher's Manual (2 volumes), Orientation Handbook and DVDs, class set (30 Student Response Books, Assessment Resource Book), and 19 trade books

Available separately:

Classroom materials without trade books	MM2-TP5
Teacher's Manual, vol. 1	MM2-TM5-V1
Teacher's Manual, vol. 2	MM2-TM5-V2
Replacement class set	MM2-RCS5
CD-ROM Grade 5 Reproducible Materials	MM2-CDR5
Trade book set (19 books)	MM2-TBS5

Grade 6

Complete Classroom Package　　　　**MM2-CP6**

Contents: Teacher's Manual (2 volumes), Orientation Handbook and DVDs, class set (30 Student Response Books, Assessment Resource Book), and 18 trade books

Available separately:

Classroom materials without trade books	MM2-TP6
Teacher's Manual, vol. 1	MM2-TM6-V1
Teacher's Manual, vol. 2	MM2-TM6-V2
Replacement class set	MM2-RCS5
CD-ROM Grade 6 Reproducible Materials	MM2-CDR6
Trade book set (18 books)	MM2-TBS6

Ordering Information:

To order call 800.666.7270 * fax 510.842.0348
log on to www.devstu.org * e-mail pubs@devstu.org

Or Mail Your Order to:

Developmental Studies Center * Publications Department
2000 Embarcadero, Suite 305 * Oakland, CA 94606-5300

DEVELOPMENTAL STUDIES CENTER™